The Country Kitchen
HERBS
Anne Chapman

The Country Kitchen

HERBS

Anne Chapman

HARLAXTON
PUBLISHING

Front and back of jacket: A basketful of fresh herbs gathered straight from a country garden in the early morning.

Front and back endpapers: An old-fashioned country kitchen with the preparation for a spicy fruit cake in the foreground. The wood burning stove is wonderful for long, slow cooking.

Page 2: Pots of herbs grow happily on a wrought-iron stand against a sunny wall.

COOK'S NOTES: Standard spoon and cup measurements are used in all recipes. All spoon measurements are level.

All ovens should be preheated to the specified temperature.
Fresh herbs are used unless otherwise stated. If they are unavailable, use half the quantity of dried herbs. Use freshly ground black pepper whenever pepper is used; add salt and pepper to taste. Flour unless otherwise stated, means all-purpose flour.

Published by Harlaxton Publishing Ltd
2 Avenue Road, Grantham, Lincolnshire, NG31 6TA, United Kingdom.
A Member of the Weldon International Group of Companies.

First published in 1992.
Reprinted in 1993.

© Copyright Harlaxton Publishing Ltd
© Copyright design Harlaxton Publishing Ltd

Publishing Manager: Robin Burgess
Project Coordinator: Barbara Beckett
Designer & Illustrator : Barbara Beckett
Photographer: Ray Jarratt
Editor in United Kingdom: Alison Leach
Typeset in United Kingdom: Seller's, Grantham
Produced in Singapore by Imago

British Library Cataloguing-in-Publication data.
A catalogue record for this book is available from the British Library.
Title: Country Kitchen Series: Herbs
ISBN:1 85837 000 0

CONTENTS

COOKING WITH HERBS

THE HERBS I have described in this book are the herbs I grow most regularly. I am lucky to live in a warm climate, with plenty of sunlight. Some of the herbs grow in pots; others grow in profusion all over. It is not uncommon for me to find basil beside a rose bush, parsley next to the daisies, and sage by the lavender. I find it a visual delight as I wander around contemplating which herb to put with roast chicken that night and deciding on the ingredients of a herb soup and a minty banana dessert.

Every herb seems to have a special affinity with a certain food – basil with tomato, mint with lamb, fennel with fish, chives with potatoes, and so on. Herbs enliven familiar dishes and enable you to change the flavor by simply changing the herb. It's fun to substitute herbs and experiment to find your own combination. Mixtures of herbs can vary; indeed, sometimes they have to if certain herbs are not in season.

Flavoring is a very individual art. Eye, taste, intuition and experience determine how to flavor a dish. It is certainly something worth cultivating if you are adventurous. No amount of flavor, however, can disguise bad cooking or poor ingredients. Flavor has to develop along with basic cooking skills. The important thing is not what flavoring is but the harmony of the ingredients complementing the main ingredient. Trust your own palate. Approach food, recipes and flavorings with curiosity and inventiveness. When you are an experienced cook, a recipe will just be an outline from which to create your own dish.

The recipes in this book are for fresh herbs, which are infinitely superior to dried ones. As most herbs are easy to grow in pots as well as in the earth, it's not difficult to have some fresh herbs always at hand. If you must use dried herbs, halve the quantity.

Herbs are used in cooking and in some medication. In fact, many began as the latter or oils, essences and perfumes–even love potions. Thyme, bay leaves and rosemary were used in the past as strewing herbs to give a house a clean smell. They are the original disinfectants.

Spices are dried herbs made from the leaves, stalks, roots, seeds, buds, bark or berries of the many various aromatic plants that nearly always originated in Asia. The spice trade from Asia to Europe began more than five thousand years ago. Herbs and spices, with their invaluable uses, have been so important to trade that wars have been fought over them.

Storing Herbs

Herbs will keep in the refrigerator for two weeks if they are fresh. Wash and dry them, and store them in plastic bags or airtight containers.

They can be frozen successfully. Choose the freshest leaves, wash them thoroughly, then blanch them by pouring boiling water over them in a strainer. Dry them in a clean dish cloth and seal them in plastic or foil packages in recipe-size quantities. Don't forget to label and date the packages.

Herbs can be stored dried. The faster they dry, the better, dry them in a microwave or oven. Spread the herbs on a paper towel on a baking sheet and place it in a very slow oven overnight. In a microwave oven they will take about 5 minutes. When cool, put them in screw-top jars and label and seal.

A decorative way of drying herbs is to hang them in bunches. If you live in an area where air isn't too polluted, simply hang them in a cool, dry position.

*The herbs in this yard are so at home and well nour-
ished they have self-seeded between the cracks in the
bricks.*

BASIL

Provençale chicken cooked in wine with garlic, olives and basil.

ONE of the great culinary herbs, basil originally came from India and was considered a royal plant. Countries like Greece, Italy and France took it up, and many of their dishes are influenced by its pungent flavor. It is considered a symbol of fertility in Mediterranean regions.

Basil is an annual and is easy to grow. It is a companion plant to tomatoes in the earth and in the kitchen. Tomato and basil complement each other perfectly.

Basil leaves go well in salads, with cheese and egg dishes, with rice, pasta and pizzas, in soups and stews, and with fish, chicken and lamb. Basil can safely replace cilantro and mint in recipes that specify those herbs.

8

Rice with Basil & Cheese

A very simple Italian dish of fragrant basil and melted cheese.

1 1/2   cups arborio rice
2   tablespoons butter, cut into small pieces
2   tablespoons finely chopped basil leaves
1   cup mozzarella cheese, grated
1/2   cup parmesan cheese, grated

Bring 3 cups of water to a boil, add salt to taste, then add the rice. Stir once and put a close-fitting lid on the saucepan. Turn the heat down low and cook for 20 minutes or until the rice has absorbed the water.

Put the cooked rice in a warm serving bowl. Fluff it up and mix in the butter and basil. Add the mozzarella and parmesan and mix quickly, as the heat of the rice melts the cheese. Serve immediately.

Guacamole with Basil

A Mexican dish, this is a wonderful starter to a meal as a dip with bread or tortilla chips.

2   large ripe avocados,
    peeled and mashed
1   green chili, finely chopped
    Juice of half a lemon
    Salt and pepper
1   garlic clove, chopped
2   tablespoons finely chopped basil leaves
    Olive oil

Combine avocados, chili, lemon juice, salt and pepper, garlic and basil then mix well. Pour in a few drops of olive oil until smooth and thick.

Provençale Chicken

A magnificent chicken dish from the south of France.

1   3-pound chicken
2   tablespoons olive oil
2   cups dry white wine
3   garlic cloves
4   tomatoes, peeled and chopped
2   tablespoons black olives, pitted
2   tablespoons finely chopped basil leaves
    Salt and pepper

Cut the chicken into 10 pieces. Heat the oil in a large saucepan and brown the chicken well on all sides. Add the wine, garlic, tomatoes, olives, half the basil, salt and pepper to taste. Cover and simmer for 20 minutes or until tender. Sprinkle the remainder of the basil over the chicken and serve. Serves 4-5.

Pesto

PESTO is one of the most wonderful herb mixtures ever created. Usually served with pasta, it can be used to stuff tomatoes, add flavoring to bean soup, or as a topping for jacket potatoes.

2   cups basil leaves, chopped
3   garlic cloves
3   tablespoons pine nuts
3   tablespoons grated parmesan cheese
3-4   tablespoons olive oil
      Pepper

Put basil, garlic and pine nuts into a food processor and blend to a thick paste. Add the parmesan. Now slowly add olive oil, blending it between drops. The sauce gradually becomes thick and smooth. Season with pepper.

It can be made the same way with a pestle and mortar.

Pesto can be stored in the refrigerator, with a covering of olive oil.

BAY LEAVES

THE BAY LEAF is a culinary herb that can be used successfully fresh or dried. Though not strictly a herb, it is so essential to French and most European cooking that it must be included here. The tree is easy to grow in a sunny place. The leaves are best used 2 days after they are picked. Throw out the tired old leaves from packages.

The bay tree is a kind of laurel which came originally from Asia. The foliage was used by the ancient Greeks and Romans to make a symbol of wisdom and glory, "crown of laurels".

The sweet, resinous aroma of bay leaf will enhance any marinade, stock, soup or stew, boiled meats and terrines, fish, vegetable and rice dishes, as well as flavor ice-creams and custards.

Fish Kebabs

The bay leaves protect the fish and add their oil to the flavor of the fish.

4	whiting fillets (or similar)
	Bay leaves
	Salt and pepper
	Juice of 1 lemon
1 1/2	tablespoons olive oil

Cut whiting into large bite-size pieces. Thread them on 4 skewers, alternating the fish with the bay leaves. Place the kebabs in a gratin dish and sprinkle with salt and pepper, lemon juice and olive oil. Marinate until time to cook them over hot coals, or under a broiler. Baste with the leftover marinade. Serves 4.

Roast Pork with Bay Leaves

A succulent pork dish penetrated with the aromatic flavor of bay leaves. The skin of the pork is removed for this dish.

1 1/2	tablespoons butter
1 1/2	tablespoons olive oil
2	pounds pork loin, boneless and tied
	Salt and pepper
10	bay leaves
1/3	cup red wine vinegar
1	cup white wine

Put butter and oil together in a heavy pot just large enough to contain the meat. Brown the meat well on all sides, then add salt and pepper to taste, bay leaves, vinegar and water. Bring to a boil, stirring the liquid, then turn heat down very low, cover tightly and cook for about 2 hours or until the pork is very tender. Check occasionally in case the liquid is drying up – add a little water if necessary.

Put the pork on a warm platter, surrounded by the bay leaves. Skim the fat from the sauce, then bring remaining juice to a boil, adding a little more wine if there isn't enough juice. Spoon the sauce over the pork and serve.
Serves 6.

Roast pork with bay leaves is an aromatic dish. Cooked this way, the pork is tender and succulent and subtle of flavor. Serve the meat juices with the fat removed.

Barbecued Steak

The small end of rump steak is the sweetest and tastiest piece of steak for broiling. Cook in one piece and then slice to serve when done.

1	*large piece of rump steak,*
	1 1/2 inches thick
1	*tablespoon olive oil*
1	*tablespoon crushed peppercorns*
	Bay leaves
	Salt

Put steak in a dish and pour the oil and peppercorns over it. Let it marinate for several hours. Turn once.

When coals of the barbecue are ready, put a layer of bay leaves on top of the rump and turn it over as it is placed on the rack so that the bay leaves protect the steak from the fire. Now put a layer of leaves on the top of the steak. Seal both sides of the meat for 2 minutes each and then turn again twice only. When the surface is firm and the meat springs back when touched, it is done.

Put on a warm platter and leave to stand for 15 minutes to relax sinews of the meat. Remove the bay leaves and slice the steak crossways. Serve with the meat juices and Dijon mustard.

VARIATION: The steak is nearly as tasty cooked in a ridged skillet on the stove. Cook exactly the same way.

CHERVIL

CHERVIL is a small biennial herb with a delicate fern-like leaf. It originated in southern Russia and the Middle East and is now native all over Europe. It grows to about 18 inches high and should be pruned to encourage growth. It likes moisture and semi-shade.

Chervil tastes a little like parsley, but more delicate, and slightly like aniseed. It is one of the most important herbs in French cooking. It is a usual herb in *fines herbes*. Chervil is best used at the end of cooking. It is wonderful with all egg dishes, fish and seafood, meats, salads, sauces and vegetables.

Chervil Soup

This old country-style soup from Belgium brings out the delicate flavor of chervil.

1	*tablespoon butter*
1	*cup potato, peeled and diced*
1	*leek, sliced*
1	*small onion, sliced*
5	*cups chicken stock*
1	*tablespoon cornstarch*
2	*tablespoons milk*
	Salt and pepper
1 1/2	*tablespoons finely chopped chervil*

Melt butter in a saucepan and add the potato, leek and onion. Cook, stirring gently, until the onion is soft. Add the stock and simmer for 30 minutes.

Put the mixture through a food processor and return to the saucepan. Place over low heat. Mix the cornstarch with the milk and add to the soup to thicken it. Season to taste.

Just before serving, add the chervil. Serves 4-6.

Broiled Veal Chops

A simple but elegant dish. Serve with waxy potatoes and a green salad.

4	veal chops
	Salt and pepper
1 1/2	tablespoons butter
1	tablespoon chervil

Sprinkle pepper on the chops and broil them for 3 minutes each side or until cooked to your taste. Add salt to taste when cooked.

Mix the butter and chervil to a smooth paste. Place the veal chops on a warm platter, dot with the chervil butter and serve. Serves 4.

VARIATION: The chervil butter is just as delicious with broiled lamb chops.

Lamb with Herb Crust

1	rack of lamb, trimmed of fat
1	cup soft bread crumbs
1/2	cup finely chopped chervil
1	garlic clove, finely chopped
2	tablespoons Dijon mustard
1	tablespoon olive oil
	Salt and pepper

Preheat oven to 400°F. Combine the bread crumbs, chervil, garlic, mustard, oil, salt and pepper. Coat both sides of the rack of lamb with the mixture; it will form a crust to seal the meat. Place the lamb on a rack in a roasting pan and put it in the oven. It should be ready in 20 to 30 minutes depending on how pink you like the meat. Serves 2-3.

CHIVES

CHIVES belong to the onion family but have a much more delicate flavor. They grow easily in the sun and need moisture and top dressing twice a year. Cut them off with scissors.

Chives are an ideal garnish, particularly for

egg dishes, cottage and cream cheeses; sprinkle on soups, potatoes, carrots and salads.

Potato Salad

Waxy potatoes are best for this salad, as they will hold their shape and absorb the dressing.

2	pounds waxy potatoes
1	tablespoon white wine vinegar
3	tablespoons olive oil
1	tablespoon Dijon mustard
	Salt and pepper
2	onions, chopped
2	tablespoons chopped chives

Boil or steam the potatoes until they are slightly underdone. Peel them immediately and cut into thick slices. Mix together the vinegar, oil, mustard, salt and pepper. Pour this mixture over the potatoes and add the onions and half the chives while the potatoes are still warm. Sprinkle the rest of the chives on when serving.

Chive Cream Cheese

This is an excellent dip to serve with crackers or crusty herb bread.

1   cup cottage cheese
1   cup yogurt
1 1/2   tablespoons finely chopped chives
1   garlic clove, finely chopped
     Pepper

Blend cottage cheese and yogurt in a blender. Mix all ingredients together well and refrigerate until serving.

The chives in the foreground have just finished flowering and scattering their seeds for new growth.

Scrambled Eggs

4   eggs
1   tablespoon chopped chives
   Salt and pepper
2   tablespoons butter

Break the eggs into a bowl and mix, but not too much. Add chives, salt and pepper. Heat the butter in a saucepan and pour in egg mixture. Leave to cook, just tilting the pan now and then. As the eggs thicken and while still 'runny', remove from heat and gently scramble with a wooden spoon. They are ready when they are still a bit 'runny'. Serve immediately.

CILANTRO

CILANTRO is a hardy annual grown for its bright green leaves and its seed. Cilantro has been used in cooking and medication for thousands of years. It is mentioned in the Old Testament and recorded in India and China. It is sometimes called 'Chinese parsley'.

Cilantro is one of the most commonly used herbs in Asia, Middle East and South America. It is the basis of many curries, spicy sauces, fresh chutneys and salads.

Cilantro & Rice Soup

Fresh herbs and spices harmonize well in this soup from India.

1	tablespoon oil
1	tablespoon chopped scallions
1	teaspoon finely chopped ginger root
1	teaspoon ground coriander seeds
1	teaspoon ground cumin seeds
6	cups chicken stock
	Juice of half a lemon
1	red chili
	Salt and pepper
1	cup long-grain rice, washed
1	tablespoon flour
1	cup yogurt
3	tablespoons cilantro leaves

Heat oil in a saucepan and add scallions, ginger, cilantro and cumin. Stir for a few minutes and then add chicken stock, lemon juice, chili, salt and pepper. Bring to a boil and add the rice. Cover the saucepan and simmer for 20 minutes.

When rice is cooked, mix flour and yogurt together and gradually add to the soup. It will thicken up. Do not boil. The flour prevents the yogurt from curdling. Stir for 5 minutes and serve with cilantro leaves on top. Serves 4.

Corn Bread with Cilantro

This is a soda bread and very simple and fast to make. It is delicious eaten warm.

2	corn cobs
2	cups wholewheat flour
2	cups flour
2	teaspoons salt
2	teaspoons sugar
1	teaspoon bicarbonate of soda
3/4	teaspoon baking powder
1	tablespoon butter
1/2	cup finely chopped cilantro leaves
1 1/2	cups buttermilk

Take husks and silk off the corn cobs and slice off the kernels. Strain the juice from the kernels by pressing hard in a sieve.

Sift flours, salt, sugar, soda and baking powder into a large bowl. Rub the butter in until the mixture resembles bread crumbs. Stir in the cilantro and then the buttermilk and mix to a soft dough.

Place on a greased baking sheet and, with floured hands, form into an 8 inch round. Use a sharp, floured knife to cut a 1/2-inch deep cross in the top of the dough. Bake in an oven preheated to 375°F for 45 minutes or until the loaf sounds hollow when tapped on the base.

Cilantro Chicken

Cilantro chicken is a very simple spicy dish to make if you have previously prepared the garam masala.

This spicy chicken is cooked on a bed of cilantro and yogurt. It is simply delicious. I include a recipe for garam masala, as it is superior to the bought kind. It will keep up to 6 months in an airtight bottle in the refrigerator.

1	chicken (free range if possible)
2	onions, chopped
2	cups cilantro, chopped

4	garlic cloves
1	tablespoon chopped ginger root
1/2	tablespoon olive oil
	Juice of half a lemon
1	teaspoon turmeric
	Salt
4	red chilies
1	cup yogurt
2	tomatoes, peeled and chopped

FOR THE GARAM MASALA

4	tablespoons coriander seeds
1	tablespoon black peppercorns
3	tablespoons cumin seeds
1	tablespoon cardamom pods
4	cinnamon sticks
1	teaspoon cloves
1	nutmeg, finely grated

Make garam masala first. Dry roast all the seeds except the nutmeg in a small pan. Roast spices one at a time. When their fragrance is released, they are ready. Take the seeds out of the cardamom pods. Blend all the seeds to a powder. Add the nutmeg and mix well.

Cut chicken into 10 pieces. Take off all the fat and skin. Put in the food processor onions, cilantro, garlic and ginger. Blend to a pulp.

Heat oil in a large saucepan and put in the herb mixture. Stir for a minute or two, then add lemon juice, turmeric, garam masala, salt, red chilies, yogurt and tomatoes. Stir for another 5 minutes, then add the chicken pieces. Coat them with the herb mixture and stir for a few minutes. Turn down the heat, put a tight-fitting lid on the saucepan and simmer for an hour. Serves 4-5.

VARIATION: Lamb is just as nice in this herb sauce. Cut it into bite-sized pieces. Serve with spicy yellow rice and a yogurt salad.

DILL

DILL is grown for its seeds and its leaves. Although it originated in southern Europe, it heavily influenced Scandinavian, German, Russian and Balkan cooking. It is an annual and easy to grow from seed.

Dill has a delicate flavor resembling caraway. It transforms cucumbers into the popular dill pickles. It is especially good with fish, cream cheese, potatoes and carrots and as a garnish for casseroles.

Broiled Trout with Dill Butter

The dill and Pernod in this dish make it absolutely delicious. Remember to put in extra salt, because trout is a freshwater fish. Serves 4.

4	whole small trout, cleaned
1	cup dill,finely, chopped
1	cup parsley, finely chopped
	Zest of 1 lemon
2	teaspoons salt
	Pepper
2	tablespoons oil

FOR THE DILL BUTTER

2	tablespoons wine vinegar
3	tablespoons Pernod
2 1/2	tablespoons butter, cut into small pieces
3	tablespoons chopped dill

Clean the trout and pat dry with paper towel. Combine the dill, parsley, lemon zest, salt and pepper. Stuff the trout with the herb mixture. Sew up the fish or fasten with a steel skewer. Brush with the oil.

TO MAKE THE BUTTER. Put vinegar in a pan and boil for a few minutes, remove from heat and add the Pernod. Now add the butter, piece by piece, stirring all the time. Add the dill.

Put the trout under a broiler, turn a few times

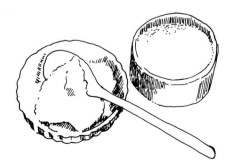

while cooking, basting with oil. They should be ready in about 15 to 20 minutes. Trout are better undercooked than overcooked. Split the trout open and pour the dill butter over the flesh. Serve with boiled waxy potatoes.

Cucumber Soup

A refreshing chilled soup for a hot summer day.

4   cups peeled, chopped English cucumber
1   onion, chopped
3   cups chicken stock
      A bouquet garni (p. 44)
      including dill and lemon peel
      Salt and pepper
1   cup yogurt or sour cream
1   cup dill, chopped
2   scallions, finely chopped

Put half the cucumber and onion in a saucepan with the chicken stock, bouquet garni, salt and pepper. Bring to a boil and simmer for 15 minutes. Remove the bouquet garni and blend the soup in a food processor. Put the soup in a tureen and let it cool. Put the remainder of the cucumber and yogurt or sour cream in a food processor and blend until smooth. Add to the soup and stir in dill and scallions. Refrigerate until ready to serve. Serves 6.

Cottage Cheese & Dill Dip

2   cups cottage cheese
1   tablespoon yogurt
2   tablespoons finely chopped dill
2   scallions, finely chopped
      Pepper

Blend cottage cheese with the yogurt in a food processor until smooth. Mix all the ingredients well together. Refrigerate until serving.

Carrots with Dill

Carrots and dill go particularly well together. Adding spices makes plain food such as chops or broiled chicken a special dish.

2   tablespoons vegetable oil
1/2   teaspoon cumin seeds
1   tablespoon finely chopped ginger root
2   green chilies
2   cups carrots, chopped
1   teaspoon coriander seeds, ground
1   teaspoon turmeric
1   cup dill, chopped
      Salt and pepper

Heat oil in a pan and add the cumin seeds and then the ginger and chilies. Keep stirring for a few minutes and then add the carrots, coriander and turmeric. Stir for a minute and add the dill, salt and pepper. Stir again, reduce the heat and cover, simmering until the carrots are done. Remove the carrots with a slotted spoon. Serves 4.

FENNEL

FENNEL is a tall, hardy perennial which grows wild in temperate climates. The fresh fronds are used as a herb, the seeds are aromatic and used to flavor pickles, biscuits and fish, the stalks of fennel are dried and used as a base to cook on. Florence fennel is grown for its bulb, which is used as a cooked vegetable and in salads.

Fennel tastes strongly of aniseed. The fronds or leaves are an accompaniment to fish and pork, either as a sauce or to cook with it. Finely chopped, it is used as a garnish to soups, salads and casseroles.

Fennel Chicken

This is a country-style chicken dish from Italy. The fennel flavors the chicken in a most subtle and delicious way.

10	*fennel stalks*
6	*bay leaves*
1	*large free-range chicken*
3	*garlic cloves*
	A strip of lemon peel
1	*cup pancetta (or bacon), finely chopped*
	Pepper
2	*tablespoons butter, cut into small pieces*
3	*tablespoons brandy*

Line the bottom of a casserole in which you will bake the chicken with the fennel stalks and bay leaves. Clean and pat dry the chicken and stuff it with the garlic, lemon, pancetta or bacon and some pepper. Lay the chicken on its side on top of the herbs in the casserole. Sprinkle the butter over it and grind some more pepper over the outside of the chicken. Cover and put in an oven preheated to 400°F.

Cook for 30 minutes and then turn the chicken on its other side, basting with the butter. Cook a further 30 minutes and then turn the chicken breast-upwards. Cook uncovered for another 15 minutes or until it is cooked and golden-brown. Remove from the oven and put over a low heat on the stove.

Warm the brandy, ignite, and quickly and carefully pour it over the fennel and chicken. When the flames have died down, transfer the fennel stalks and bay leaves with the chicken on top to a warm serving dish.

Skim the fat off the meat juices. Cook the liquid for another 3 or 4 minutes, stirring all the while. Serve this sauce separately. Serve the pancetta or bacon pieces with the chicken.

Fish Flamed in Fennel

A whole fish is broiled over a bed of fennel sticks, then ignited.

1	large whole fish, gutted and cleaned
	Juice and peel of 1 lemon
	Dry fennel stalks
	Salt and pepper
2	tablespoons olive oil

Pat the fish dry. Stuff the lemon peel and fennel stalk into the fish. Marinate the fish with salt and pepper, oil and lemon juice.

Lay the fennel stalks in a shallow flameproof dish. Lay the fish over the fennel and pour half the marinade over it. Put under the broiler for 7 minutes, then turn, marinate and broil the other side for 10 minutes or until cooked.

Take from under the broiler. Set the fennel alight. The smoky fennel flavor enhances the fish flavor very subtly.

Carrot Salad

Choose the fine new shoots of the fennel for this wonderful, simple salad.

2	tablespoons finely chopped fennel leaves
2	tablespoons olive oil
1	teaspoon lemon juice
1	teaspoon Dijon mustard
	Salt and pepper
1	pound carrots

Combine fennel, oil, lemon juice, mustard, salt and pepper in a screw-top jar and shake well. Grate the carrots, then pour the vinaigrette over them, mixing gently. Refrigerate until needed.

The barbecue is perfect for cooking fish flamed in fennel.

GARLIC

GARLIC belongs to the same family as the onion and it is just as highly regarded. It is used every day for cooking all over Europe, the Middle East, Asia and South America. In a moderate climate it can be grown from a bulb.

Garlic is extremely good for you. Apart from its antiseptic qualities, it is thought to be beneficial in the treatment of various ailments. Garlic can make the dullest dish interesting. Cooked garlic is not as strongly flavored as raw garlic and can be safely eaten. Chew parsley to neutralize garlic breath. Press on the garlic cloves with a broad knife to release the aroma and make them easy to peel.

To list all the ways to use garlic would be impossible. Essential in curries delicious in chutneys it will enhance most savory dishes.

Garlic Lamb

This is an old French peasant way of cooking lamb. It takes a long time to cook but is well worth the effort–the meat is so tender, a knife is hardly needed to cut it. Serve with lentils and brussels sprouts.

1	leg of lamb
1	tablespoon butter
1	tablespoon olive oil
2	teaspoons sugar
1	cup white wine
1	cup hot water
	Salt and pepper
6	small onions, peeled
3	carrots, sliced
6	garlic cloves
	A bouquet garni (p. 44)

Trim fat off the lamb. Heat the butter and oil in a heavy pan. Brown the meat on all sides, then add sugar, wine and water. Season with pepper. Add whole onions, carrots, garlic, bouquet garni and salt. Lower the heat, cover, and simmer for 5 hours, turning the meat over a few times.

Transfer the meat and onions to a warm platter. Strain the liquid to remove the fat. Reduce the sauce by half. Pour a little over the lamb and serve the rest separately. Serves 8.

Garlic Soup

Don't be frightened off by the large quantity of garlic. Cooked this way it loses its pungency and becomes surprisingly mild. This is a rich country soup from the south-west of France.

2	cups chicken stock
6	cups water
	A bouquet garni (p. 44)
2	tablespoons goose fat or butter
24	garlic cloves, peeled
	Salt and pepper
1	teaspoon grated nutmeg
3	eggs, separated
6	slices stale bread
2	tablespoons olive oil

Bring stock, water, and bouquet garni to a boil. Remove from heat. Melt the goose fat or butter in a saucepan and add the garlic cloves. Cook gently, and just before they brown pour the stock over them. Add the salt, pepper and nutmeg and cook for 15 minutes. Blend in a food processor and return to the saucepan.

Spread the egg whites on the slices of bread and toast in the oven.

Beat the egg yolks and olive oil together. Add a little soup to the egg mixture, then gradually pour the mixture into the soup, stirring all the time. Do not let it boil again.

To serve, put a slice of bread in each soup bowl and ladle over the garlic soup. Serves 6.

Chicken with Garlic

I first ate this dish in Thailand. It was so delicious I have attempted to emulate it here. Cooked on a barbecue, it is even nicer. Serve with rice or baked sweet potatoes.

1	large free-range chicken
10	garlic cloves
1	teaspoon salt
2	tablespoons coconut cream
1	red chili, chopped
1	tablespoon pepper
1	cup cilantro, chopped
1	cup mint, chopped
	Juice of 1 lemon

Cut the chicken into 10 pieces. Mix all the other ingredients together to make the marinade. Rub the marinade into the chicken and leave to marinate for 12 hours if possible.

Cook the chicken pieces on a rack under a very hot broiler. Turn every 5 minutes until the chicken is tender.

Garlic soup is a real country-style dish, and surprisingly subtle.

Overleaf: I gathered and composed this nasturtium and mint salad one Sunday morning while wandering around a country garden. Feel free to use your imagination with salad combinations.

MARJORAM

My version of the northern European dish, mock hare. Albrecht Dürer's classic study of a hare is in the background.

MARJORAM is a perennial and, in warm climates, is very easy to grow. It has a delicate perfume, so it is wise to add it just before the end of cooking. An extremely versatile herb, marjoram can be used as a substitute for thyme. Also, the two herbs go together very well. Oregano (p. 29) is the wild variety.

Marjoram is a favorite herb for poultry stuffings; it makes delicious sandwiches with cream cheese; goes well with salads, omelets, sauces, vinegars, pizzas, meat loaves and sausages and with poultry, pork and veal.

Crumbed Green Beans

A dear friend cooks her beans this way. They are deliciously crunchy.

1	pound green beans
1	tablespoon butter
3	tablespoons soft white bread crumbs
1	tablespoon marjoram

Mock Hare

A traditional Sunday dish from the north of Germany. It is often shaped into the form of a sleeping hare. It's fun to shape, and it gives the meat loaf more interest. Use your cat as a model, remembering to change the ears. Shape as an egg first, the smaller end being the head.

1	pound lean beef, ground
1	pound lean pork, ground
4	eggs, beaten
2	onions, finely chopped
1	leek, finely chopped
2	cups soft bread crumbs
2	tablespoons marjoram
3	juniper berries, crushed
	Salt and pepper
1	teaspoon paprika

Combine all the ingredients in a bowl and mix thoroughly.

Attempt to shape your hare. If you give up, you can just mold it into a long roll. Place on a greased baking sheet and cook in a preheated oven at 350°F for about 1 hour. It is cooked when the outside is golden-brown and, when pierced with a skewer, red meat juices do not flow.

Serve with gravy made with the meat juices that will flow out of the meat, a little flour, wine and water. Mashed potatoes and parsnips go well with mock hare.

Trim the tops off the beans and otherwise leave whole. Cook in boiling water for about 10 minutes; they should be still a bit crisp and not soft. Drain.

Melt the butter in the saucepan and stir in the bread crumbs; keep stirring until they are almost golden. Put the beans back in, along with the marjoram. Stir for a minute or two to warm the beans, and serve.

Onion & Olive Pizza

Pizzas can be made with all sorts of combinations of toppings. This one is very simple and fast. It is more like pizzas that would have been made a hundred years ago, as it is made in a pan on top of the stove. It has a firm, crunchy texture rather like a cracker. There isn't any yeast in the dough. This pizza is 7 inches across.

1	cup flour
1	teaspoon salt
1	teaspoon baking powder
3	tablespoons water
3	tablespoons olive oil
4	onions, finely sliced
15	black olives, pitted and halved
1	tablespoon marjoram
	Salt and pepper

Sift the flour, salt and baking powder in a mound on a board. Make a well and put in 2 tablespoons of cold water. Make a dough, adding a little water when necessary. Knead it for a few minutes, then roll it out in a round about 7 inches in diameter.

Heat half the olive oil in a pan and add the onions. Cook until soft and golden. Remove from heat.

Heat the rest of the oil in a heavy pan and when very hot put the round of dough in. Adjust the oil so that it comes just to the top of the dough. Cook for 5 minutes on a medium heat; when the underside is golden, turn it over.

Now, very quickly spread the onion slices over the crust, place the olives in circles on top, and scatter the marjoram evenly. Season with salt and pepper. Cover the pan and cook for another 5 minutes or until it is ready. Serve immediately.

Serves 4 as a starter, 2 as a main meal.

MINT

MINT has a very fresh, clean taste and perfume. Mints are perennial, but their foliage dies away in winter. They are grown by propagation and need rich soil, plenty of water and partial shade. There are many varieties from Asia as well as Europe, but the most common varieties for culinary use are the round-leaved mints, which include apple mint, spearmint and bergamot.

Mints have traditionally been used as a medicine to cure all sorts of diseases. In Asia, the Middle East and Britain, mint is one of the most common herbs. It makes a wonderful salad herb. Lamb marries happily with mints. Mint can be used with fruit such as oranges, bananas and pineapples. It goes well with carrots, potatoes, peas and beans, lentils, tomatoes and eggplant. In Asia it is often used in curries, fresh salads and chutneys.

Mint is a very easy herb to grow and it's well worth growing a pot or two.

Pineapple & Mint

1	pineapple
2	tablespoons finely chopped mint
3	tablespoons superfine sugar
	Juice of 2 oranges
2	tablespoons kirsch

Peel and cut pineapple into small pieces. Do this over a bowl, so you don't lose the juice. Strain the juice into a saucepan with the mint, sugar and orange juice. Bring to a boil and simmer for a few minutes. Add the kirsch when the mixture cools down. Pour the liquid over the pineapple pieces. Refrigerate. Serve sprinkled with sprigs of mint.

Minty Meat Balls

Delicious meat balls from Albania. Mint is almost the national flavor, it is so popular.

1	pound lean ground lamb
2	eggs, beaten
2	garlic cloves, crushed
3	tablespoons finely chopped mint
1	teaspoon cinnamon
1/4	teaspoon cayenne
	Salt and pepper
1/2	cup olive oil

Combine all ingredients except the oil in a mixing bowl and knead until smooth. Leave for 2 hours, covered, in the refrigerator.

Shape the meat mixture into smooth balls. Heat the oil and fry the meat balls a few at a time until they are brown all over. Keep them warm in a hot serving dish. Serve with hot potato salad, coleslaw and a jar of pickles. Serves 4.

OREGANO is the wild variety of marjoram and has a much more pungent and powerful flavor. It is easy to grow in well-drained soil and a sunny position.

Oregano is very important in Italian and Greek cooking and is excellent with tomatoes, cheese, beans, zucchini, eggplant, fish, beef, and pizzas.

Spaghetti alla Rustica

3   tablespoons olive oil
2   garlic cloves, crushed and chopped
2   tablespoons rinsed and chopped
     anchovy fillets
2   tablespoons finely chopped oregano
1   pound spaghetti
2   tablespoons finely chopped parsley
     Pepper
     Parmesan cheese, freshly grated

Heat the oil in a pan and put in the garlic and anchovies. Stir them until combined and add the oregano. Remove from heat.

Meanwhile, cook the spaghetti in a large pan of boiling water. Drain and put into a warm bowl. Add the anchovy mixture, the parsley and pepper. Stir and serve immediately with a bowl of parmesan. Serves 4.

Nasturtium & Mint Salad

     Tiny spinach leaves
     Tiny cos lettuce leaves
1   cucumber, sliced
1   carrot, sliced
     Cherry tomatoes
     Apple mint leaves, whole
     Nasturtium flowers and leaves

VINAIGRETTE
3   tablespoons olive oil
     Juice of half a lemon
1   garlic clove, crushed
     Salt and pepper

Arrange all salad ingredients attractively in a salad bowl. Put the vinaigrette ingredients in a screw-top jar and shake until mixed. Dress the salad at the table.

Barbecued Oregano Shrimp

Keeping the shells and heads on may seem a little fiddly, but shrimp retain the most flavor if they are kept in their shells, and the flavor is absolutely worth it.

2	pints green shrimp
1/2	cup vegetable oil
	Pepper
1	tablespoon finely chopped oregano
	Juice of 1 lemon
2	scallions, finely chopped
6	scallions, cut in 1-inch lengths
	Sprigs of oregano

Prepare shrimp by running a sharp knife along the back to pierce the shells and flesh, then devein them and wash thoroughly, but keep the heads on and the shells almost intact.

Mix together the marinade of oil, pepper, oregano, lemon juice and chopped scallions. Put the prepared shrimp into the marinade, making sure some gets inside the shells. Marinate for at least 2 hours.

Thread the shrimp onto skewers, alternating with scallions and sprigs of oregano. Put them on the barbecue for 5 to 10 minutes depending on their size, turning several times and brushing with marinade. Serves 4-6.

VARIATION: This dish can be made just as simply under a broiler or stir-fried in a wok with chili-flavored oil.

Oregano and chives are flourishing in these beautiful terracotta pots against a background of flowering rosemary.

Mushrooms Oregano

A simply made dish which can be eaten hot or cold as a salad or as an accompaniment to meat dishes.

2	tablespoons olive oil
1	pound small button mushrooms
2	teaspoons salt
2	garlic cloves, chopped
1	tablespoon oregano
	Juice of half a lemon
	Pepper

PARSLEY

Heat the oil in a pan and add the mushrooms. Cook for a minute, then add the salt. Cook, stirring, for 5 minutes then add the garlic, oregano, lemon juice and pepper. Mix well. Remove from heat as soon as the mushrooms soften.

PARSLEY is the most widely known of herbs all over the world. It has been used for thousands of years as a medicine as well as a flavoring. It is a biennial and easy to grow in fairly rich soil and a sunny position. The most common varieties are the curly-leaved and the flat-leaved, sometimes known as Italian parsley.

It is packed with vitamins A, B, C and considered a general tonic by some people. As a culinary herb it is indispensable for bouquet garni and *fines herbes*, it adds flavor to mashed potatoes, salads, eggs, sandwiches, stuffings, vegetables and sauces–in fact, almost all savory dishes.

Tabbouleh Salad

This delicious, pungent salad of parsley and mint is traditionally served in individual bowls with lettuce leaves or vine leaves to scoop up the salad.

1	cup fine burghul (cracked wheat)
3	tablespoons finely chopped scallions
1 1/2	cups parsley, finely chopped
1/2	cup finely chopped mint
1	tomato, peeled and finely chopped
3	tablespoons olive oil
1	tablespoon lemon juice
	Salt and pepper
	Lettuce or vine leaves

First soak the burghul in water for 30 minutes. Drain and dry.

Combine the burghul, scallions, parsley, mint, tomato, oil and lemon juice. Add salt and pepper to taste. Serve with the leaves.

VARIATION: Garnish with black olives.

Barley Soup with Parsley

A really old-fashioned hearty soup. The lamb adds a sweet taste.

1/2	cup split peas
2	onions, chopped
	A bouquet garni (p. 44)
1	cup barley
	A piece of neck of lamb, trimmed of fat
2 1/4	quarts water
	Salt and pepper
3	carrots, chopped
1	rutabaga, chopped
3	parsnips, chopped
1	cup parsley, chopped
3	tablespoons chopped parsley

Put split peas in a bowl and pour boiling water over them. Leave to stand for an hour to soften. Drain.

Into a large saucepan put the peas, onions, bouquet garni, barley, lamb, water, salt and pepper. Bring to a boil, cover and simmer for an hour. Add the carrots, rutabaga, parsnips and a cup of parsley and simmer 45 to 60 minutes until all the vegetables are soft. Serve with the extra parsley sprinkled on top. Serves 6-8.

Green Sauce

This French sauce is excellent for serving with any meat or fish dish, hot or cold. Make it just before serving, and be sure the egg yolk is really fresh.

1	egg yolk
1	tablespoon Dijon mustard
1	cup olive oil
2	tablespoons lemon juice
	Salt and pepper
2	tablespoons freshly chopped parsley
1	tablespoon freshly chopped tarragon
1	tablespoon freshly chopped chives
1	tablespoon freshly chopped chervil

Put egg yolk in a bowl along with the mustard. Mix and gradually add the oil drop by drop as you do when making mayonnaise. Stir in the lemon juice at the end and add pepper and salt and the parsley, tarragon, chives and chervil.

An old country dish, parsleyed ham (jambon persillé) is a refreshing meat dish for a special-occasion summer lunch.

Parsleyed Ham (Jambon Persillé)

2	cups chicken stock
2	cups dry white wine
3	pound cooked ham
	Pepper
4	juniper berries, crushed
3	tablespoons gelatin
1	cup parsley, finely chopped
2	tablespoons white wine vinegar

Put stock and wine into a saucepan and bring to a boil. Add the ham, some pepper and the juniper berries and simmer for 30 minutes or until the ham is tender.

Take the ham out and reserve the hot liquid. Either cut the ham into bite-sized pieces or flake it, pulling it apart with your fingers. Put the pieces into a bowl or a terrine.

Soften gelatin in a little cold water and then stir into the hot liquid. When it is dissolved, allow the liquid to cool. Add the parsley and vinegar and pour over the ham. Leave to set in the refrigerator.

To serve, unmold from the bowl or serve it in the terrine.

ROSEMARY

Spring lamb with rosemary is a special dish to cook for a celebratory lunch or dinner.

ROSEMARY is a very hardy evergreen bush with pale blue flowers and spiky leaves. It is very aromatic and smells something like pine needles. It will grow in any warm place. It is the herb of remembrance which soldiers in Australia and New Zealand wear on Anzac Day to remember their fallen comrades. Rosemary grows wild in Turkey and the Mediterranean region. It is reputed to have medicinal virtues.

Rosemary has a great affinity with lamb, pork and chicken. It is excellent in soups and stews, with tomatoes or vegetables. It is one of the few herbs that go well with sweet dishes such as ice-cream, sorbets, cakes and puddings.

Rosemary Turnips

Serve these aromatic turnips with chicken or duck and mashed potatoes.

6	small white turnips
1 1/2	tablespoons butter
2	garlic cloves, crushed
3	sprigs rosemary

Slice the turnips. Cook them for 5 minutes in boiling water or until half-cooked. Drain.

Melt the butter in a pan and put in the turnip slices, garlic and rosemary. Keep turning them so they cook evenly. They will go a golden color.

Spring Lamb with Rosemary

2	tablespoons olive oil
1	tablespoon butter
	A small leg of lamb, trimmed of fat
3	garlic cloves, crushed
6	sprigs rosemary about 3-inches long
	Salt and pepper
2	cups dry white wine

Heat oil and butter in a large saucepan. Add the lamb, garlic and rosemary. Brown the lamb well on all sides. Add salt, pepper and 1 1/2 cups of white wine. Bring to a boil, cover and simmer for 1 1/2 to 2 hours until tender. Turn two or three times during cooking.

Transfer the lamb, sitting on the sprigs of rosemary, to a warm serving plate. Skim the fat off the cooking liquid and add the rest of the wine and water if necessary. Boil very fast for a few minutes, stirring all the while. Serve the sauce separately.

Pork & Veal Pâté

There are many variations to pâtés and terrines. It is fun to experiment with herbs and spices.

1/2	pound bacon slices
1 1/2	pounds ground lean pork
1	pound ground veal
1	onion, finely chopped
	Salt and pepper
1	teaspoon grated nutmeg
2	tablespoons chopped rosemary
2	tablespoons chopped parsley
2	garlic cloves, chopped

Remove rind from the bacon and line a terrine or loaf pan with the slices. Mix together half the pork, the veal, the onion, salt and pepper, and nutmeg. Then mix the remaining pork with the herbs, garlic and some salt and pepper.

Put half the pork and veal mixture into the terrine in a smooth layer, then add the pork and herb mixture. Finally add the remaining pork and veal mixture.

Cover the terrine with foil and put in a roasting pan with water. Place in a preheated oven at 350°F for 1 1/4 hours. Remove from the oven and place a weight on top of the terrine until it is cold. Turn out and refrigerate until serving.

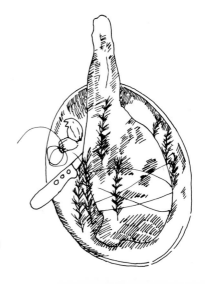

SAGE

SAGE is another old medicinal herb now used as a flavoring. The sage bush will grow for years in a sunny, well-drained position. The flavor of sage is very powerful, so care should be taken not to use too much.

It is an excellent herb to use with rich dishes like duck, goose, rabbit, pork or sausages. The Italians love it with veal and calf's liver. It is incomparably better fresh than dried.

Rabbit with Prunes

This homely dish is usually served with potatoes and brussels sprouts or red cabbage.

1	tablespoon olive oil
1	tablespoon butter
1	rabbit, cut in pieces
1	onion, sliced
1	carrot, sliced
2	garlic cloves
3	cups red wine
1	teaspoon sage
	A bouquet garni (p. 44)
3	juniper berries
	Salt and pepper
30	prunes, pitted and soaked

Melt oil and butter in a pan and brown rabbit pieces. Add the onion and carrot. Let it sweat a little, stir, then add the garlic, red wine, sage and bouquet garni. Bring to a boil and add the juniper berries and salt and pepper to taste. Cover, simmer for 1 1/4 hours or until tender.

Add the prunes for the last 15 minutes of cooking. If the sauce is very thin, drain off the liquid and reduce by boiling very fast to a thick consistency. Serves 4.

Potato Purée

A delicious sage purée to serve with pork or sausages. Nice enough to eat on its own.

2	pounds potatoes
1 1/2	teaspoons olive oil
1	onion, chopped
2	cups stock
1/2	teaspoon chopped sage
	Salt and pepper
2	tablespoons butter

Peel potatoes and boil them until tender. Put oil in a pan and when hot add the onion. Sauté until transparent. Add the stock, sage, salt and pepper and boil down to a third of the volume.

Mash the potatoes thoroughly and mix with the sage bouillon and the butter over a moderate heat. Mix to a smooth purée and serve.

Sage Biscuits

Crisp, crunchy biscuits with the delightful combination of sage and cheddar. They are great to hand around with pre-lunch drinks.

2	cups flour
1	tablespoon baking powder
2	tablespoons butter, cut into sticks
1/2	cup cheddar cheese, grated
2	tablespoons finely chopped sage
1/4	teaspoon cayenne
3/4	cup milk

Sift flour and baking powder into a large bowl. Put butter and cheese into the flour and blend until it resembles bread crumbs. Add the sage and cayenne. Stir in some of the milk and mix, adding more as needed. Knead dough lightly on a floured board and roll out to 1/4-inch thickness. Cut into rounds and place on a baking sheet, separated from each other. Bake in an oven preheated to 425°F for 15 minutes or until done.

Sage biscuits are quick and easy to make and a great favorite with my family.

TARRAGON

TARRAGON is one of the greatest of culinary herbs. There are 2 varieties, the superior being French, but probably Russian tarragon is more widespread. French tarragon is grown from root division or cuttings and likes a sunny position and light, well-drained soil.

Tarragon is an aromatic and is indispensable in *fines herbes* and sauces such as hollandaise, béarnaise and tartare. It blends wonderfully with chicken and pâtés, fish, shellfish and salads. The fresh leaf is essential, as it does not dry well. The delicate flavor enhances most savory dishes.

Sauce Tartare

This is a traditional sauce for fish. I like it with boiled meats as well, as they sometimes taste a little bland. Be sure the egg yolk is really fresh.

1	egg yolk
1	teaspoon Dijon mustard
	Salt and pepper
	Olive oil
1	tablespoon tarragon vinegar
2	teaspoons chopped tarragon
1	teaspoon chopped gherkins
2	teaspoons chopped green olives
1	teaspoon chopped capers

Put the egg yolk into a bowl with the mustard and some salt and pepper. Add oil drop by drop, stirring fast all the time until it emulsifies, then add the oil a little faster until the mixture is smooth and thick. Stir in the tarragon vinegar and add the chopped tarragon and the well-drained gherkins, olives and capers. Refrigerate until serving.

Tarragon Butter

An instant sauce to melt over meat cooked under a broiler or over a barbecue. Vegetables sautéed in the butter are excellent with the subtle taste of tarragon.

4	tablespoons butter
1	tablespoon white wine vinegar
3	tablespoons finely chopped tarragon
	Salt and pepper

Cream butter until smooth and gradually beat in the vinegar. Then add the tarragon and salt and pepper to taste. Roll the butter into a long log and cut pieces off as you need them. Keep refrigerated.

Celery with Tarragon

This celery dish can be served as a dish on its own or as an accompaniment to a rich meat or fish course.

4	cups celery cut into 2 1/2-inch pieces
1	tablespoon chopped tarragon
2	tablespoons chopped parsley
1	cup dry white wine
1/2	teaspoon grated nutmeg
	Salt and pepper
	Soft bread crumbs
2	tablespoons butter, cut into little sticks

Put the celery in a saucepan and cover with the herbs, wine and stock, nutmeg, and salt and pepper to taste. Bring to a boil, cover, and simmer for 15 minutes.

Arrange the celery on a gratin dish. Pour the herb liquid over it, sprinkle with bread crumbs and the butter. Bake for 30 minutes in a preheated oven at 350°F. Serve.

Tarragon Chicken

1   chicken, free-range if possible
1/2   cup tarragon leaves
1 1/2 tablespoons diced pancetta or bacon
         Salt and pepper
2   tablespoons butter
2   carrots, thinly sliced
2   onions, thinly sliced
3   cups hot water
1   tablespoon chopped tarragon

Wash and dry the chicken. Gently pull away
skin near the breast and legs and insert some of
the tarragon leaves on either side. Put the rest in
the cavity along with pancetta or bacon, salt
and pepper.

Melt the butter in a baking dish, add the carrots, onions and put the chicken on top of the
vegetables. Cover and cook for 20 minutes in a
preheated oven at 300°F. Add hot water and
some salt and pepper then cover again. Turn up
the oven to 400°F and cook for a further 50 minutes or until tender.

Put the chicken on a serving dish and keep
warm. Strain vegetables off the cooking liquid
and remove the fat. Add the chopped tarragon
and boil down to half the quantity or until it is
thick, stirring from time to time. Serve the sauce
separately.

*VARIATION: Add a dash of port or madeira to
the sauce when the chopped tarragon is added.*

THYME

THYME is a powerful aromatic and one of the
essential culinary herbs. It is grown by root division and requires a sunny position and light,
well-drained soil. The most popular thymes are
garden thyme, lemon thyme and caraway
thyme. It has a pungent and warming aroma
and taste.

Thyme is indispensable in bouquet garni,
fines herbes and stuffings and is a background
to many stews and soups of meat, fish and vegetables. It is a good roasting herb with lamb,
beef, pork, poultry and game. Fresh thyme is
much superior to dried.

Pork Chops with Apple & Thyme

4   pork chops
1/2   tablespoon chopped thyme
         Pepper
1   tablespoon olive oil
1   teaspoon wine vinegar
1   tablespoon butter
2   cooking apples, sliced
1/4   teaspoon chopped thyme

Marinate chops in the 1/2 tablespoon of thyme,
pepper, oil and vinegar for a few hours. Broil
the chops, basting with marinade occasionally.

While the chops are cooking, melt the butter,
add the apples and thyme, and sauté the apples
until soft. Serve chops and apples on warm
plates.

Thyme Stew with Dumplings

An old-fashioned stew just like Grandma used to make. Dumplings are so delicious and easy to make I don't know why they have gone out of fashion.

3	pounds chuck steak or similar
1	tablespoon flour
2	tablespoons butter
2	cups onions, chopped
2	cups stock
	Salt and pepper
1	cup carrots, chopped
1/2	cup celery, chopped
1	rutabaga, chopped
1	tablespoon chopped thyme

FOR THE DUMPLINGS

1	cup flour
1	teaspoon baking powder
1/2	teaspoon salt
2	tablespoons butter
1	tablespoon chopped thyme
1	tablespoon chopped parsley
1/4	cup milk

Trim fat off the steak, cut the meat into bite-sized pieces and lightly dip them in flour. Melt butter in a saucepan and add the onions and the meat. Brown the meat and onion all over. Add the stock, salt and pepper and, stirring gently, bring to a boil. Add carrots, celery, rutabaga and thyme. Stir, cover, then transfer to the oven pre-heated to 325°F and cook for 1 1/2 hours or until the meat is tender.

Meanwhile, make the dumplings. Sift the flour, salt and baking powder into a bowl and rub in the butter. Add the chopped thyme and parsley. Gradually add the milk until you get a wet dough. Makes 10 to 12 dumplings.

Twenty minutes before the stew is ready to serve, drop the dumplings into the stew. Make sure they sit on top of pieces of meat and not in the gravy. Cover and simmer for 20 minutes.

Serve with mashed turnips or parsnips.

Opposite: A very simple dish, baked thyme vegetables looks wonderful on the table and tastes just as good.

Baked Thyme Vegetables

A lovely vegetable dish to accompany a roast or as a meal in itself. It is rather like a vegetable pie without the crust.

2	tablespoons olive oil
1	cup onions, sliced
4	medium zucchini, sliced
2	garlic cloves, crushed
2	teaspoons chopped thyme
	Salt and pepper
2	small eggplants, sliced
4	medium tomatoes, sliced
3	tablespoons grated gruyère cheese

Rub a gratin dish with oil and spread the onion slices evenly on it. Make a layer of zucchini and cover with a little garlic, thyme, salt and pepper. Add the eggplant and then the tomato. Sprinkle the rest of the garlic, thyme and some salt and pepper over the dish. Sprinkle the olive oil over it and then the cheese. Bake in a preheated oven 350°F for 45 to 60 minutes until the vegetables are cooked.

WATERCRESS

THE pungent flavor and brilliant color of watercress make it highly regarded as a culinary herb. It grows in or near water, from seed or by propagation. If you pick wild watercress, make sure the water isn't polluted. Store it in a bucket of fresh water.

Watercress is cooked as a vegetable the same way as spinach and accompanies roast and broiled meats and poultry. It is excellent as a salad and an ingredient in *fines herbes*. The flavor enhances soup, egg dishes, sauces and sandwiches.

Watercress & Potato Soup

A simple but classic soup from France. The cream transforms the soup into the luxury class.

1 1/2 quarts water
2 1/2 cups potato, diced
1   cup watercress leaves
6   tablespoons heavy cream
1/2   teaspoon grated nutmeg
       Salt and pepper

Bring water to a boil in a large saucepan, add the diced potato and cook until soft. Drain and mash the potato or put through a food processor. Put the purée back into the water and add the watercress. Bring to a boil and simmer for 10 minutes. Add the cream and keep simmering, stirring constantly for about 5 minutes. Add the nutmeg, and salt and pepper to taste. Serve with some sprigs of watercress on top. Serves 4.

VARIATION: Mix a cup of yogurt with a tablespoon of flour and substitute for the cream.

WATERCRESS SALADS

Here are four ways of making watercress salad. They are excellent with rich meat dishes; their peppery flavor adds a lightness to the meal.

Grapefruit & Hazelnut

1   large bunch watercress,
       trimmed and washed
3   tablespoons hazelnuts
FOR THE VINAIGRETTE
       Juice of half a grapefruit
2   tablespoons olive oil
       Salt and pepper

Make vinaigrette by putting into a screw-top jar the grapefruit juice, oil, salt and pepper and shaking well. Put the watercress into the salad bowl with the roughly chopped hazelnuts and toss the vinaigrette over the salad. Mix and serve immediately.

Beets & Olives

1   bunch watercress, trimmed and washed
1   cup diced cooked beets
1   tablespoon pitted olives
FOR THE VINAIGRETTE
2   tablespoons olive oil
1   teaspoon lemon juice
       Salt and pepper

Mix oil, lemon juice, salt, pepper and shake. Toss with the watercress, beets and olives at the table.

VARIATION: ORANGE
As above, but substitute 2 oranges, peeled, sliced finely and halved, for the beets and olives.

VARIATION: APPLE
Substitute 2 sliced apples for the beets and olives, and add 1/2 teaspoon of roasted cumin seeds and a dash of cayenne to the vinaigrette.

Shrimp with Watercress

| 2 | pints cooked shrimp, shells and veins removed |
| 1 | cup watercress leaves, chopped |

FOR THE VINAIGRETTE

3	tablespoons olive oil
2	tablespoons lemon juice
2	tablespoons Dijon mustard
	Salt and pepper
12	watercress sprigs

Combine vinaigrette ingredients in a screw-top jar and shake well. Pour the dressing over the shrimp. Serve with a few sprigs of watercress-enough for a few per portion.

Watercress salad with beets and olives is a simple but delicious salad to serve with a rich main course.

MIXED HERBS

FINES HERBES

Fines herbes is a French term for the subtle mixture of parsley, chives, tarragon and chervil. The herbs are finely chopped together and used as a garnish for soups, egg dishes, sauces, and vegetable, fish and meat dishes. The mixture of herbs can vary-watercress makes an excellent addition.

Fines Herbes Butter

3/4 cup unsalted butter
2 tablespoons fines herbes
(1/2 tablespoon each of parsley,
 chives, tarragon, chervil finely chopped)
1 1/2 teaspoon lemon juice

Mix the butter, herbs and lemon juice thoroughly. Form into a large roll and keep in the refrigerator to use as needed. Use it instead of a sauce to garnish fish and meat and toss with peas, new potatoes or any other vegetable.

VARIATION: Add watercress, finely chopped, garlic or scallions.

BOUQUET GARNI

A bouquet garni is a little bunch of herbs tied together which is used to flavor stocks, soups and casseroles.

The classic bouquet garni is a couple of bay leaves and some sprigs of thyme and parsley tied together with string. A piece of carrot and a few celery tops are sometimes included; rosemary or tarragon can be added for chicken or lamb; stalks of fennel and lemon peel are ideal for fish dishes; orange peel goes well with hearty beef dishes. The bouquet is discarded before the dish is served.

Mixed Herb Stuffings

Herbs make a wonderfully aromatic stuffing mixed with bread or ground meats. Whether stuffed into chicken or turkey, cabbage or tomatoes, they enhance each other's flavor.

Chicken Stuffing

1 1/2 cups stale bread, crusts cut off
1/2 cup milk
1/3 cup onions, diced and lightly fried
1 cup fines herbes (this page)
1 egg
 Salt and pepper

Put the bread in a bowl and pour the milk over. Mix together; bread will become soft crumbs. Add remaining ingredients and mix well.

Pork & Herb Stuffing

This is excellent for stuffing cabbage leaves, peppers, eggplants, zucchini and tomatoes.

2   tablespoons butter
2   tablespoons finely chopped onion
3   garlic cloves, chopped
3/4 pound lean ground pork
1   cup stale bread, crusts cut off
1/2 cup milk
3   tablespoons fines herbes (p. 44)
    Salt and pepper

Melt butter in a saucepan and add the onions. When soft, put in the garlic and ground pork and stir until the meat is lightly cooked.

Put the bread in a bowl and pour milk over it. Knead until it is soft, then add all the herbs, salt and pepper, and the onion, garlic and pork mixture. Mix well. Spoon into vegetables.

Rice Stuffing

1   cup onion, finely chopped
2   garlic cloves, chopped
2   tablespoons olive oil
2   cups cooked rice
1   cup water
3   tablespoons fines herbes (p. 44)
1/2 teaspoon ground cinnamon
1/2 cup sultanas
    Salt and pepper

Cook onion and garlic in the oil until the onion is soft. Stir in the rice. Add the water gradually when needed. Add the rest of the ingredients and mix well. Cook until the water has evaporated, about 15 minutes.

VARIATION: Add 2 tablespoons of chopped dried apricots which have been soaked in water for an hour.

Rice stuffing tastes equally good stuffed into poultry or vegetables such as zucchini, peppers and tomatoes.

Herb Sandwiches

There is no need to have butter on these delicious herb sandwiches.

4	tablespoons cottage cheese
1	tablespoon milk
	Salt and pepper
1	cup fines herbes (p. 44)
12	slices of bread, crusts trimmed off

Put cottage cheese and milk into a food processor and blend until smooth. Mix with the herbs, salt and pepper. Spread on the bread and cut sandwiches into fingers or triangles.

VARIATION: Add ham or shredded chicken for a thicker sandwich; replace cottage cheese and milk with an avocado and a tablespoon of lemon juice; add chopped walnuts or olives.

Spicy Potato Filling for Pitta Bread

Pitta tastes much nicer warm, so put it in the oven or under the broiler.

2	large potatoes, cooked and mashed
2	scallions, chopped
2	tablespoons chopped cilantro
1	tablespoon chopped mint
1	tablespoon lemon juice
1/4	teaspoon cayenne
1	teaspoon ground coriander seeds
1	teaspoon ground ginger
	Salt

Combine all the ingredients and mix well.

Simple and delicious, spicy potato filling for pitta bread makes an extra special snack or lunch.

Pasta with herbs makes a simple homely lunch.

Herb Omelet
(Omelette aux Fines Herbes)

A classic omelet cooked in the French manner with the eggs still a bit 'runny' on the inside. Speed is essential, so do not take your eyes off it while cooking.

8	eggs
4	tablespoons finely chopped fines herbes
	(p. 44)
1 1/2	teaspoons butter
	Salt and pepper

Beat eggs and add the *fines herbes* and half the butter in small pieces. Add salt and pepper.

Melt the rest of the butter in a pan; add the eggs. In just 30 seconds, start lifting the edges of the omelet so that the liquid egg will start seeping under.

When the underneath is lightly browned, fold the omelet in two and serve. Serves 4.

Pasta with Herbs

1	pound fresh tagliatelle
1	cup cream
1/4	cup butter
2	tablespoons finely chopped oregano
2	tablespoons finely chopped chives
3	tablespoons finely chopped parsley
2	garlic cloves, chopped
1/2	teaspoon grated nutmeg
	Salt and pepper
	Freshly grated parmesan cheese

Put pasta into plenty of boiling water and cook for 6 minutes. At the same time, heat the cream gently in a pan with half the butter. Stir the herbs into the cream along with the garlic and salt and pepper.

Drain the pasta and put into a warm serving bowl. Pour the cream mixture over the pasta and mix well. Put the remaining butter, cut into sticks, on the top with a sprinkling of parmesan and serve immediately. Serves 4.

INDEX

Page numbers in **bold** type indicate illustrations.